PROCEEDINGS

OF THE

DEMOCRATIC

STATE CONVENTION,

HELD AT COLUMBUS, OHIO,

FRIDAY, JULY 4, 1862.

CONTAINING THE SPEECHES OF

HON. SAMUEL MEDARY, HON. C. L. VALLANDIGHAM, HON. RUFUS P. RANNEY, AND HON. ALLEN G. THURMAN.

THE ADDRESS AND PLATFORM,

BALLOTINGS FOR CANDIDATES, AND NAMES OF DELEGATES IN ATTENDANCE.

DAYTON:
FROM THE PRESS OF THE DAYTON EMPIRE.
1862.

DEMOCRATIC STATE CONVENTION,

COLUMBUS, JULY 4, 1862.

BEFORE THE CONVENTION.

For several days before the Convention, Delegates and Democrats from various portions of the State, began flocking to the Capital, in such numbers that by Thursday noon, the registers of the Hotels bore testimony to the fact that more had arrived then than were delegates in the Convention. That afternoon and during the following night, every train arriving brought delegations of tens, twenties, fifties, and in some instances as high as hundreds, and it was admitted by all, Republicans as well as Democrats, that the Convention was the largest of the kind ever held in the State.

At 11 o'clock, on the night before the Convention, the special train, bringing the delegation from the Third District, some five hundred and fifty, accompanied by the "Regimental Band" of Dayton, arrived, and the delegation marched to the Goodale House, where their Representative in Congress, Mr. Vallandigham was stopping, and gave him a handsome serenade, to which he responded in a brief and patriotic speech, which was listened to and applauded by the thousands of Democrats assembled from every section of the State.

THE CONVENTION.

MORNING SESSION.

It having been announced that the Convention would assemble at Naughton's New Hall, (the largest in the City,) it was crowded to its utmost capacity at an early hour, accommodating not more than one fourth or one fifth of those who desired to attend.

At 10 o'clock the Convention was called to order by WAYNE GRISWOLD, Esq., Chairman of the Democratic State Committee, when, upon motion of Dr. STOUT, Hon. JOHN O'NEIL, of Muskingum, was elected Temporary President, who, upon being conducted to the Chair, thanked the members of the Convention in a brief and eloquent manner, for the honor conferred upon him.

Judge OAKLEY CASE, of Hocking county, on motion of W. C. GOULD, Esq. was appointed temporary Secretary, and Messrs. FRANK H. HURD, of Knox, A. R. VAN CLEAF, of Warren, and LEWIS GLESSNER, of Hancock, were appointed Assistant Temporary Secretaries.

The following Committeemen were hen named by the various Districts:

COMMITTEE ON CREDENTIALS.

IST.	DIST.
lst John Connell,	11th Levi Dungan,
?d H. O. Gilbert,	12th A. L. Perrill,
?d J. McElwee,	13th John O'Neill,
lth J. L. Winner,	14th J. J. Jacobs,
ith C. R. Mott,	15th J. S. Way,
ith N. A. Devore,	16th B. F. Helwick,
'th J. H. Thomas,	17th J. H. Wallace,
ith H. T. Van Fleet,	18th J. F. Hughes,
th W. L. Cole,	19th A. J. Ross.
th M. R. Willett,	

OMMITTEE ON PERMANENT ORGANIZATION, RULES, AND ORDER OF BUSINESS.

IST.	DIST.
st G. W. Martin,	11th John Frazee,
d George Ritt,	12th P. Overmeyer,
d G. W. Stokes,	13th L. E. Moss,
th J. Counts,	14th George Rex,
th William Sawyer,	15th J. C. Clark,
th Benjamin Flora,	16th B. F. Spriggs,
th J. G. Dunn,	17th J. H. Trainer,
th M. May,	18th C. Hanks,
th C. B. Stickney.	19th W. B. Dawson.
h H. S. Beaver,	

COMMITTEE ON RESOLUTIONS.

ST.	DIST.
t A. G. W. Carter,	11th B. F. Coates,
l Robert Moore,	12th P. Van Trump,
l C. L. Vallandigham,	13th George B. Smythe,
h J. F. McKinney,	14th J. A. Estill,
h William Gribben,	15th S. A. Miller,
h John Johnston,	16th J H. Heaton,
h A. G. Thurman,	17th Samuel Lahm,
h T. W. Bartley,	18th R. P. Ranney,
h George E. Seney,	19th M. Burchard.
h M. Handy,	

MMITTEE TO SELECT A STATE CENTRAL COMMITTEE.

T.	DIST,
; George Fries,	11th Edward Rains
R. K. Cox, jr.,	12th Thomas Wilson,
W. J. Gilmore,	13th Frank H. Hurd,
ı W. A. Purtlebaugh,	14th John B. Young,
ı Benj. Linsey,	15th W. R. Golden,
: J. C. Hayes,	16th C N. Allen,
ı W. M. Stark,	17th Calvin Ferrall,
ı J. A. Bebee,	18th M. L. Root,
ı Thomas Beer,	19th Daniel B Wood.
ı F. Johnson,	

On motion of Hon. WM D. MORGAN, Licking, the following resolution was opted:

esolved, That all resolutions offered in the Conven-, be referred, at once and without debate, to the imittee on Resolutions.

On motion, the Convention then ad-rned to meet at half past 1 o'clock, P. , in the State House grounds, in order t the thousands of Democrats present ght be enabled to participate in and ness the proceedings of the Convention.

AFTERNOON SESSION.

The President, Mr. O'NEIL, called the nvention to order at half-past 1 o clock, and announced that that body was ready to hear the reports of Committees, when J. J. JACOBS, Esq., of Ashland, submitted the following

REPORT OF THE COMMITTEE ON CREDENTIALS.

"Your committee would respectfully report, that they have examined the credentials which were placed in their hands, and find that all the counties of the State are fully represented. The names of the delegates entitled to seats in the Convention are given in the list which is herewith placed at your disposal."

LIST OF DELEGATES' NAMES BY COUNTIES.

Adams County—Dr. B F Coates, D S Eyler, Nathan Hawk, J P Patterson, W E Hopkins, J T Copeland.

Allen—James McKenzie, C N Lamison, J H Merty, Wm Armstrong, M W Vance, Jno Eaton, Wm Dowling, Geo M Baxter, W C Hanger, D S Fisher.

Ashland—Paul Oliver, John Taylor, John Charles, Henry Blust, G W Hill, J J Jacobs, Mr. Richenbach, John Van Nest, James Hamilton, Josiah Thomas, H S See, J McCool, H S Knapp, T J Kenney, H Hamilton.

Ashtabula—F S Smith.

Athens—W R Golden, Mr Warren.

Aug aize—Col. Wm Sawyer, A A Trimble, H B Kelly, E P Howell, Chas Boesel, R B Gorden.

Belmont—J H Heaton, M J W Glover, I R Cline, Jesse Barton, John M Gardner, Ross J Alexander, J T Collins, Geo H Umstead, Jno Cross, H R Brown, S M Howey, J R Mitchel.

Brown—C A White, N A Devore, Jno Mitchell, D G Devore, F Handman, David Toshell, John G Doren.

Butler—P Wright, Robert Christy, J Agnew, A Stewart, Dr. Corson, S Dearmond, J Kemp, James Clarke, and a large number of advisory delegates.

Carroll—Calvin Ferral, John K Bowers.

Champaign—Nathaniel Seeva, W A Durtlebaugh, Alfred A Hull, David Loudenbach.

Clark—John H Bloss, James V Ballentine, John Meranda, L Hudgell, John Keifer, Finley Shartle, Hugh Hagan, John Coffield, John J Forbes, Giles Gordon, Dr Curtiss, Wm Rowan, Major H Hough, Samuel Bowius, Cornelius Gram, F Coblentz, Mathias Bruner, Matthew Bonner, Newton Conway, Geo Duke, L Schaffer, J H Myers, David Shaffer, Wm Werden, John Thomas, John Rohrer, J H Thomas.

Clermont—John Johnston, N M Tribble, R M Griffith, N L Teal, R L McKinley, S R Hamilton, Joseph Beckings.

Clinton—B Hinkson, James W Ferran, Jacob Theobald, Joseph Roff, A Jones, T I Carothers.

Columbiana—James S Seetin, T S Hays, T S Woods, J H Wallace.

Coshocton—William Sample, Charles Hoy, Lewis D Moss, Henry Metham, John T Simmons.

Crawford—David Ogden, Robert Lee, Samuel Hoyt, Dr. A Jenner, John Newman, Ed Cooper, Wm Pope, Charles Kepplinger, Edmund Kepplinger, Ed Ferrill, William Ferrill, Andrew Dickson, Wm Cummings, W F A Corey, James Dickson, W McMannis, Wm Miller, Joseph Worden, A M Jackson, Dr. Fulton, D Cahill, C M Dodson, Thos Beer, A Apenbeimer, A Shonert, S Sporr, A Fulton, B Morris, Thos Shawk, Wils Stewart, A Barnes, John Franz, Wm Trimble, A A Rahl, J Shawke; T Creighton, Jas Flickinger, J Mallenhopt, Hugh Corey, John Welch, Esq. Hutty, J Welch, A S Reisinger, Daniel Riblett, J M McEwen, L Jackson, L J Reed, M Buchman, J Herr, J Van Voorhies.

Cuyahoga—R P Ranney, Asa B Paine, D P Rhodes, J M Hughes, A Hughes.

Darke—John L Winner, I B Price, Lloyd Brown, Jesse Woods, Thos Teal Geo Dively, Wm Falkner, Cornelius Brown, Wm Hughes, John Noggle, Job B Miller, D Hogan, Martin Marker, F Kruenick, S J Licklider, John Stultz, Wm Wight, Dr. Hager, Sam'l Arnold, Aaron Beckelhimer, George Poe, Peter Shook, N S York, John Coppess, J Townsend, P H Kilbourne,

Michael Mead, George Jenkinson, David Smith, John Grissom, G W Ringer, Jacob Weller, Andrew Coppess, Geo D Medford, Solomon Marker, Joseph G Brush, Stephen Shepherd, Dr. Wm Matchett, B Fulker.

Defiance—John Widol, J J Tanyhill, H Casad.

Delaware—Thos Bennett, John Nash, —— Poppleton, J R Klapp, Thomas Mann, A J Smith, Robert Wilson.

Erie—G S Patterson, J D Lea, S P Stowe, J M Brown.

Fairfield—Wm Medill, P Van Trump, B W Carlisle, Joseph Sharp, W Whaley, A D Benedum, D Dawson, W Schopp, A C Stout, T Duncan, C Trovinger, J M Hickle, J C Rainey, and a large number of advisory delegates.

Fayette—W H Stewart, Scott Harrison, James F Ely, John C Hayes, James W Farran.

Franklin—Samuel Medary, A G Thurman, Jacob Reinhard, George W Manypenny, A G Hibbs, A W Taylor, John Chaney, B C Kinney, J O Reamy, R Brooks, F Compton.

Fulton—S H Cotely, M Handy.

Gallia—R Brown, P Murphy, W Verran.

Geauga—Charles W Brown.

Greene—Wm M Stark, S Hart, J Jewett, John Day, S Murphy, Wm. Jones, Martin Berry, Wm Brock, and a large number of advisory delegates.

Guernsey—Clark Rose, S Shafner, J W White, Henry McCleary, Lewis Baker, S B Drummond, T B Lawrence, J C Hunter, John Brown.

Hamilton—G Stephens, John Conley, A G W Carter, Geo Fries, J Clements, A Schoonmaker, John Ridgway, H Jessup, John Smith, J Bean, N Hoefer, P Linck, E H Johnson, H O Gilbert, C Ross, R K Cox, Thos Stevens, Joe Smith, John Martin, Robt Moore, G W Cunningham, John Schnell, John Gise, John Smith, W Ward.

Hancock—L Glessner, G C Bund, C E Jorden, Wm Porterfield, W W Siddell, A B Shorer, H S Burson, Solomon Shofer, Wm Gribben.

Hardin—Jas M White, A W Graham, O B Hoppersett, A S Ramsey, G S Williams, P C Boslow, P S Letson, M W Van Fleet, R S Cutts, W A Kelly, W H Munnell, John H Geary.

Harrison—P Donahue, S Holmes, Will Wiley, E Johnson, N S Hanna, J M Paul, J Ramsey, C N Allen.

Henry—James Brannan, J C Jaqua.

Highland—Benjamin Flora, W W Malcomb, J M Trimble, J M Hughes, A L Hurts, Edward Johnson, Samuel Pike.

Hocking—Dennis McCarty, Oakley Case, Manning Stiers, W C Gould.

Holmes—John H Westman, D P Leadbetter, John Varneck, N M Louthan, L R Critchfield, E Estill, J A Estill, S M Hebron, R M Cameron.

Huron—A G Post, C B Stickney, F W Graves, Abijah Ives, W W Redfield, James A Jones.

Jackson—Levi Dungan, Joseph Aten, John Sanders,

Jefferson—James McKinney, John H Trainer, John V Smith.

Knox—L Harper, F H Hurd, A B Ink, John Boggs, James Honey, Jerome Presley.

Lake—M L Root, Oliver Andrews.

Lawrence—J A Scott, L Anderson.

Licking—Geo B Smythe, Wm D Morgan, G Atherton, Wm Pare, A M Stewart, W F Preston, James H Grant, James M Tompkins.

Logan—Hanson Thomas, Luther Smith, Sidney B Foster, Benj Oder, Ben E Shumake, James S Robb, Jonathan Woodward, W V Marquis.

Lorain—E F Peck, D Belden, Dr. Langdon, E Byington, John B Robinson, Geo C Underhill.

Lucas—F Johnson, A L Backus, W W Howe, V Colburn, John Isham, F Warren, L B Lathrop.

Madison—John Dunn, Jesse M Linson.

Mahoning—S W Gilson, John Cessna, James Mackey, W B Dawson.

Marion—J M Christian, H T Van Fleet, T H Hodder, H Osborne, Wm Vricket, E K Corban, Wm H C Moore, John Rozencrantz, C Knowles, John Hebermann, David Eustie, Michael Durtt, John O Regan, C Hobbman, H Vankirk, C Sager, John Thompson, John Sowers, Hiram Miley, Wm Dennis, R Wang.

Medina—John B Young, W F Hess, Thomas White.

Meigs—A Condee, R McKay, J Radford.

Mercer—F C Le Blond, Wm E Baker, Benj Linsey, Hiram Murlin.

Miami—Jonas Ward, T L P Defrees, Vachel Shipley, W J Downs, Geo W Blessington, J J Solomon, Christian Leaner, Martin Gance, John Smith, J F McKinney.

Monroe—J S Way, John Keyser, Israel D Riley, J Spriggs, J B Williams, Matthew Brown.

Montgomery—C L Vallandigham, F L Scheu[illegible], T Lowe, S B Smith, Wm Stansel, J Mumma, G Kenned[illegible] Wm Ramsey, J Decker, Judge Morse, Isaac Voorhee[illegible] Dr. J Berlin, John Hoover, Jesse Harry, Jesse Wogman, John Cusick, Eli James, Daniel Riter, Jacob Kuhns, John W Turner, Adam [illegible]by, Dr. Hawkin[illegible] Theo P Eby, Henry Wise, Wm [illegible]gler, John Wenge[illegible] Jacob Kunkle, Dr. Kemp, Joshua Oram, John Alle[illegible] Jacob Brenner, George Kemp, James Kelly, Daniel Snyder, P Long, jr., [illegible] T Beals, George S Gebha[illegible] Fred H Hoover, Geo A Grove, Wm Leichty, Elias Leggett, Z Catrow, J F Kern, John Reed, Lewis Meas[illegible] Seymour Yeaze[illegible], Dr. Shanefelt, J F Thompson, Es[illegible] Moyer, Esq., Musselman, Jacob [illegible]ter, Geo Olinge[illegible] Hiram Lewis, Michael Wallace, John Bellville, Dr. Alexander, R G McEwen, Robert Miskelly, M Swadene[illegible] J F Bollmeyer, I H Cole, F Fisher, Harvey Blanchar[illegible] S F Woodsom, W N Love, T F Thresher, Levi Wolls[illegible]ton, Dr. J A Walters, John P Dietz, D A Houk, W Gillespie, John C Cain, B M Ayres, Amos Decke[illegible] George Wogaman, Abraham Cahill, John P Klin[illegible] Philip Waltz, Henry Kline, P A Lafee, Wm Wamb[illegible] Wm Dickey, John L Miller, John Minick, Antho[illegible] Stephens, Joseph Clayton, Adam Snyder, N E Jorda[illegible] W H Bellville, D K Boyer, D A Houk, J H Cush[illegible] Hugh Wiggim, Dennis Dwyer, Jonathan Kenney, Edward Conway, John Stephans, George Hochwalt, C. Auber, J H Stoppelman, E O'Brien, John Reeves, H Richmond, W W Kenney, D W Reese, R M Du[illegible] John Colhauer, Conrad Schenck, Geo D Kinder, Pet[illegible] Long, sr., W T Logan, T M John, Nicholas Staley, Fr[illegible] Reichstetter, George White, Hamilton Turner, G Houk, Dr. Kelso, Joseph Zwisler, George McCain, a[illegible] one hundred and five others.

Morgan—John E Hanna, C McGlashan, J C Clar[illegible] Arthur Taggart, R Silvey.

Morrow—J A Beebe, Byram Beers, G L Salsbur[illegible] Lester Bartlett, J Commins, Seth Cook, Henry Fore[illegible] Joseph Morris, Isaac Lefever, Hiram Linnell.

Muskingum—Elias Ellis, F H Jennings, John O'Nei[illegible] Samuel Adams, J M Stout, Wm Pringle, R M Cro[illegible] Geo Lawhead, and a large number of advisory delegates,

Noble—Wm Clymer, Edward Burson, J P Gill, B Spriggs.

Ottawa—W L Cole, James Park, Henry Hobbeler.

Paulding—H Horey, C M Dodson.

Perry—Wm M Brown, Wm E Finck, W H Holde[illegible] Peter Overmyer, J J Johnson.

Pickaway—A L Perrill, Wm Hughes, Mr Julian, I Wayne Griswold.

Pike—Jacob Vallery, James Jones, John T Moo[illegible] S W Shaw, I C Jenisten, Thomas Wilson, Geo D Col[illegible] John Kent.

Portage—M A Birchard, N P Squire, A A Ross.

Preble—C J Beam, S Banta, Dr. Joseph N Mitche[illegible] Judge W J Gilmore, and a large number of adviso[illegible] delegates.

Putnam—H J Bœnmer, John Buchanan, Jno Swaze[illegible]

Richland—John Y Glessner, T W Bartley, Jo[illegible] Schrock, H W Patterson, John Coulter, H R Smit[illegible] Robert Cairnes, Jonas Smith, John A Lee, Daniel O[illegible]ings, L C Kelly, Samuel Myers, J N Allen, M May.

Ross—Alfred Yaple, R C Galbraith, Dennis Ogle, W[illegible] H Safford, Harvey Sperry.

Sandusky—John Bell, M M Coe, P Tew, C Powers, K Kill.

Scioto—A J Enslow, Wm Newman, W I Nichols, Raine.

Seneca—P H Ryan, S Bucker, A B Hooey, Samu[illegible] Wade, J J Nash, Ed Childs, Eber Higby, W W Armstrong, Alfred Landon, E T Stickney, Wm Dildin[illegible] Daniel Dildine, Wm Lang, George E Seney, G S Christif, Isaac Kagy, Rudolph Kagy, A Benham, Dr. Ruf[illegible] Norton, A Beelhay, John McCauley, W P Noble, S [illegible] Shaw, C Stener, R R Titus, Wm Smith, Philip Emic[illegible]

M P Skinner, Dr. A G Owen, George Miller, S Ireland, Seth Jaqua.

Shelby—D Stockdale, James Johnston, W W Vaughn, J Counts, James C Dryden, D L Bush, James Blue, Geo Meeker, Samuel Hutton.

Stark—Henry E Smith, Samuel Lahm, Geo W Belden, S S Geib, T W Chapman, John Herbst, John S Tiernay, A McGregor.

Summit—J D Cummins, C Hanks, George Miller

Trumbull—M Burchard, S Doughton, D B Woods.

Tuscarawas—Benj F Helwig, Robert Baker, G W Dingman, W Anderson, Samuel Barnes, F Bukey, J McElroy, J D Elliott.

Union—Col Robb, Alex. Gray, James Gardner, John Blakely, Mr. Thompson.

Van Wert—P De Puy, C W Lown, Henry Weible.

Vinton—John Frazee, A J Swaim, H C Moore, Daniel Booth, Nelson Richmond.

Warren—G W Stokes, A R Van Cleaf, D W Van Dyke, Dr W A Johnson, A S Kirby, Patrick Denny, Amos Crane, Wm F Hayner, J K Haines, H G Stansel, F S Lilly.

Washington—Wm Lorey, M D Follett, S A Miller, E Waernicke, Wm Sharp, O Tucker, Conrad Knigbaum.

Wayne—Geo Rex, A H Byers, Benj Eason, John S Brown, Wm Barton Hiram Fisher, E D Otis, J A Marchand, N Steinmetz, T J McElhenie, David Carlin, John Larwill, L D Odell, Wm Coulter, Andrew Ault, Adam Tanner, John H Oberly, Major Aquilla Wiley.

Williams—Wm Shendan, jr., M R Willett, J B Kimmel, S C Brown.

Wood—W Stewart, P McManus.

Wyandot—C R Mott, S M Worth, J M Reid, John Fouke, John Kiser, Jonathan Maffett, Henry Flock, Cyrus McCauley.

The above report was accepted and adopted, when J. M. Trainer, Esq., of Jefferson, submitted the following

REPORT FROM THE COMMITTEE ON PERMANENT ORGANIZATION, RULES, ETC.

Your committee on Permanent Organization, Rules, etc., would report as permanent officers of the Convention:

FOR PRESIDENT,

GOV. SAMUEL MEDARY, of Franklin.

FOR VICE PRESIDENTS,

Dist.
1st. B. W. Cunningham, of Hamilton.
2d. Charles Ross, of "
3d. A. R. Vancleaf, of Warren.
4th. J. Frank McKinney, of Miami.
5th. Charles Boesel, of Auglaize.
6th. John L. Hughes, of Highland.
7th. Matthias Martin, of Franklin.
8th. William Reed, of Delaware.
9th. Silas W. Shaw, of Seneca.
10th. John Buchannan, of Putnam.
11th. William Newman, of Scioto.
12th. William E. Finck, of Perry.
13th. Wm. Sample of Coshocton.
14th. Dr. Underhill, of Lorain.
15th. M. D. Follett, of Washington.
16th Ephraim Johnson, of Harrison.
17th. J. D. Cummins, of Summit.
18th. M. A. Burchard, of Portage.
19th. James McKinney, of Jefferson.

FOR PRINCIPAL SECRETARY,

AMOS LAYMAN, of Franklin.

FOR ASSISTANT SECRETARIES,

Dist.
1st. Richard Mathers, of Hamilton.
2d. Richard K. Cox, jr., of "
3d. Thomas O. Lowe, of Montgomery.
4th. Henry Miller, of Darke.
5th. J. M. White, of Hardin.
6th. John G. Doren, of Brown.
7th. David Haskall, of Madison.
8th. Thomas Hodder, of Marion.
9th. A. M. Jackson, of Crawford.
10th. R. M. Johnston, of Lucas.
11th. William E. Hopkins, of Adams.
12th. O. Case, of Hocking.
13th. Samuel Adams, of Muskingum.
14th. John Weitman, of Holmes.
15th. Cyrus McGlashan, of Morgan.
16th. Jesse D. Elliott, of Tuscarawas.
17th. Calvin Ferall, of Carroll.
18th. Arthur Hughes, of Cuyahoga.
19th. W. B. Dawson, of Mahoning.

Your committee would report the Rules of the last Democratic State Convention for the government of this. Respectfully submitted.

J. H. Trainer, Ch'n Com.

M. May, Sec'y.

The gentlemen selected by the Committee, and named in the foregoing report, were then unanimously declared to be elected officers of this Convention.

Granville W. Stokes, L. Harper and Wm. C. Gould, were appointed a committee to notify Governor Medary of his election as President of this Convention, and conduct him to the chair.

After a short absence, the Committee returned, being accompanied by Governor Medary, when the temporary Chairman introduced him to the Convention, saying:

Here in the heart of Ohio, where so long has been the residence of Governor Medary, no introduction to the Democracy of Ohio is needed. To name him is sufficient.

Repeated cheers greeted Mr. Medary, when he turned to the audience, and said:

Gentlemen, Democrats of Ohio: You must excuse me if I should appear a little nervous on being notified of the high honor you have conferred upon me. It is not often that men in modern times are promoted to high and honorable distinctions without being notified beforehand that they would be so promoted. Little did I expect, when I appeared as a delegate from Franklin county, a few minutes ago, to hear my name announced as President of this most respectable and patriotic Convention of the Democracy of Ohio. And when I say Democracy of Ohio, I hope there is nothing treasonable in that word! (Laughter and applause.) If there is nothing treasonable in the name and organization of the Democracy of the late *United* States, and I hope may be again—if there is nothing treasonable in the name or organization, there is nothing treasonable in this assembly. If you will indulge me a few moments, I will offer a few remarks. I do think this a proper meeting for the Fourth day of July. Eighty-six years after the Declaration proclaiming freedom and the rights of man to the world, I am astonished to hear men of sense casting imputations upon those old fathers who stood by their country in the hours of trial as well as prosperity, both according to the principles laid down as we understand them, and according to the great founder of Democracy, Thomas Jefferson—I say I am surprised to hear imputations cast upon those old heroes.

There is hardly an old man here who has not a son under the command of the United States forces; and we have placed our sons in the hands of him who is Commander in Chief of the armies of the Union, and who has sworn to preserve not only the country, but the liberty and freedom of its peoole.

Gentlemen, if you will permit me, I will take this opportunity to indulge in a personal remark or two. I am astonished at you, gentlemen, to-day, to have the boldness and daring to defend an old gray-haired Democrat from the charges resting upon him. In vindicating myself, I will vindicate you. [A voice "that's so."] I have been charged with not being loyal to my country. God knows that if I am not, nobody is. I have my opinions, and you might as well attempt to consolidate into one great church all the religious faith of the country, as to consolidate all the political opinions under one head, and require every man of every party to believe alike. But when I pay my taxes I support the Government. When I pay for each spoonful of sugar I put in my tea, I support my government; and when I pay for the tea my wife puts in her teapot, I support the government; when I pay for my clothes, or for my winding sheet, I support my government. But I have done more: I sent one of my sons into the army, and supported him for six months out of my own pocket, without the aid of a dollar from the government; and a son-in-law, who married one of my daughters—and you who have daughters know how they are attached to their husbands, and how you are attached to them, especially when they are left alone—was in the thickest of the fight, having charge of a regiment, when Lyon fell at Springfield. And yet I am a traitor!

Why am I called a traitor? Because I believe that the doctrines which were taught me, and which I have taught to thousands of others, are true and necessary to the welfare of the country. Has the Democratic party ever been untrue to the country? (Several voices —Never; no, nor ever will be.) They say I am a revolutionist; so I am; I was cradled by revolutionary parents. But I look to the Co stitution to guide me in the changes that con upon us.

There was a time when they would bu John Rogers at the stake, because he did n believe in their religion, and there may be time, I admit, in all governments, when m will be punished for differing with the Sta politics of the country. (A voice—"That tir has arrived, hasn't it?) I understand it h been intimated that this Convention could n and ought not to be held. For why? Because politically we differ with t administration in authority. I ask you, su posing these difficulties in the United Stat had occurred when the Democrats were power, and supposing your Democratic Pre dent and Congressmen had carried on t war for the suppression of the rebellion co trary to the feelings and opinions of their p litical opponents, would they not have sa they disapproved of it? Have they not ways said so, when we had a war on hand? Let me warn you, on this 4th of July—tl Sabbath of Liberty—that whenever the do trine is preached, that during civil war men must close their mouths till the civil co motion is put down, civil liberty is in dang Let a tyrant be elected, and civil commoti may be gotten up for the express purpose suppressing freedom of speech. (Voices That's so; that's the doctrine.) Were I ambitious man, like Napoleon or Nero, a wished to make my people support me at hazards, my first object would be to get either by my own efforts or by some otl means, civil commotions, that I might requ the people to be unanimous in my support. then might not only manage that war, bu might rob and steal to my heart's conte with my minions around me, filling their pur at the expense of the people who dare not op their mouths. (A voice—That time ne will come in this country. (Another voice "It has come already.") I say fearlessly, tl the truest friend the President and the cou try have, is he who will openly and boldly nounce the robbery of the poor soldiers in fields. But the other day, through the sec machinery of secret operations, and by closing of mouths, not only here, but up the floors of Congress, a grave Senator years' standing, in the gravest body in world, (or it once was so regarded,) was tected and exposed in selling his *influence* $50,000, for securing a contract of fifty tho and half-made muskets! And yet we are t that we and our children, and our childre children must submit to this robbery and dignity without daring to open our mouths at risk of being run off somewhere at some h of the night, when neither wife nor children can sound the alarm. Now, if there is a Republican—so-called—or a simon pure, unadulterated Union man, that is too good to pray at the feet of the old Gamaliels—if there is one such under the sound of my voice, I ask him if what I have said here to-day in the advocacy of a free expression of right and the condemnation of wrong, if it would not protect him if we got in power as much as it would protect us when you are in power? I would scorn to preach that which was good only for Democrats; I would scorn to preach a doctrine that was not as potent for the protection of my political enemies as myself and my friends. When I had a little difficulty on my hands in Kansas—a civil war in miniature exhibition—and undertook to settle the troubles there and bring society to order and peace, I was denounced bitterly by what was called the Free State papers. And when I was asked if I saw those attacks, I would reply: "Yes, and I have read them with interest and care." Every expression that gave new light, instead of being used for the imprisonment of the author, I would use to the best advantage, and let the rest go.

Gentlemen, I have said enough. (Go on—don't stop.) The subject is inexhaustible. I have asked and plead for the maintenance and continuance of the organization of this old democratic party, that I have known from my youth. In my study of revolutions, and especially such as this, and particularly the manner in which the civil part was prosecuted, I have looked for the time when we would be looked to and prayed to as the last hope of the country. If the time never should come when we could step in and save the country, the organization would do no harm, for it is a peaceable and constitutional organization.

There is nothing riotous in our party there is no thieving and lying in us, at least beyond what is natural to human nature, and not even as much as can be found in other quarters sometimes. I have believed the time would come when the whole face of this rebellion would be changed, and if it does come, I fear you, my democratic friends will be the only Union men left in the country. (A voice—They are all that are left now.) If there shall be intrigues of other nations, and the authority at Washington shall ask you to submit peaceably to the division of these States, who then will be the disloyalists and disunionists? But we will let that pass, for I fear an unhappy condition not far ahead. I received to-day a most extraordinary confidential letter, from a source but little expected, warning us that the hour—not thirty days, perhaps, distant, when it is believed that a proclamation will be issued from Washington, asking us northern people to submit to a division of this country. (Never—not a bit of it.) I ask, then, if this be the fact—and I don't pretend to state whether it is or not—who then will be in favor of the dissolution of the Union? The very men with contracts in their pockets, who have grown rich by the misfortunes of their country in this war; and they who have carried ropes to hang those who never breathed a disloyal breath, will have to give the ropes over to us. (Applause.)

I thank you, gentlemen, most heartily, for the manner in which you have honored me as President of this body; and I think that I will prove before many months, that of all men in this world, neither your President to-day, nor the men making up this Convention, are entitled to the charge of disloyalty to their country.

C. M. Allen, Esq., of Harrison county, from the Committee to select a State Central Committee, presented the following report, which was accepted and adopted:

DEMOCRATIC STATE CENTRAL COMMITTEE.

Dist.	
1st.	George Fries, Cincinnati.
2d.	R. K. Cox, Jr., Cincinnati.
3d.	J. F. Bollmeyer, Dayton.
4th.	James Moore, Bel fontaine.
5th.	David S. Fisher, Lima.
6th.	James F. Ely, Washington C. H.
7th.	John Chaney, Canal Winchester.
8th.	George L. Saulsbury, Cardington.
9th.	Abner M Jackson, Bucyrus.
10th.	Mr. Johnson, Toledo.
11th.	Wm. Newman, Portsmouth.
12th.	Wm. C. Gould, Logan, Hocking county.
13th.	Frank. H. Hurd, Mt. Vernon.
14th.	George Rex, Wooster.
15th.	John E. Hanna, McConnelsville.
16th.	Lewis H. Baker, Cambridge.
17th.	James McKinney, Steubenville.
18th.	J. D. Cummins, Akron.
19th.	Daniel B. Wood, Warren.

Hon. C. A. White, the Representative in Congress from the Brown district, offered the following resolution, which was adopted:

Resolved, That the Secretary be instructed to send a telegraphic dispatch to the President of the Democratic State Convention now in session at Harrisburg, Pennsylvania, informing him that we have the largest delegate Convention ever assembled in Ohio, every county in the State being represented; and that the utmost harmony and good feeling prevail.

THE NOMINATIONS.

On motion, the Convention proceeded to nominate candidates for the various offices.

SUPREME JUDGE.

After an informal vote by counties, the Convention unanimously nominated Rufus P. Ranney, of Cleveland, for Supreme Judge.

Messrs. Kenny, Stout and Sawyer, were appointed a Committe to notify Judge Ranney of his nomination.

SECRETARY OF STATE.

William W. Armstrong, of Seneca, was nominated by acclamation for Secretary of State.

ATTORNEY GENERAL.

For Attorney General, there were two ballotings, with the following result:

First Ballot.

Scribner	59
Spence	37
Thresher	131
Critchfield	136

Messrs. Scribner and Spence were then withdrawn.

Second Ballot.

Thresher	148
Critchfield	215

Upon the announcement of the above ballot, Mr. Thresher, of Montgomery, arose and said:

Mr. President:—The partiality of my friends having induced them to present my name to the Convention, I take this opportunity to return my heartfelt thanks to them and to the Convention for the very complimentary vote given me, and move that the nomination of Mr. Critchfield be made unanimous.

The question being put, Mr. Critchfield's nomination was made unanimous.

SCHOOL COMMISSIONER.

There were two ballotings for School Commissioner, with the following result:

First Ballot.

Johnson	24
Cathcart	181
Peacock	50
Martin	125

Messrs. Peacock and Johnson were withdrawn:

Second Ballot.

Martin	94
Cathcart	258

Charles W. H. Cathcart, of Montgomery, was declared to be nominated, and the nomination was made unanimous.

BOARD OF PUBLIC WORKS.

First Ballot.

McAboy	76
Gamble	152
Cary	63
Christian	47
Newman	34

Messrs Christian and Newman were withdrawn.

Second Ballot.

McAboy	40
Cary	33
Gamble	289

James Gamble, of Coshocton, was nominated, and the nomination made unanimous.

Judge Ranney having been notified of his nomination by the committee appointed for that purpose, appeared before the Convention desiring to decline; but it would not allow him to, so he, in a very graceful and handsome manner, accepted the nomination.

THE PLATFORM.

Judge Moore, from the Committee on Resolutions, submitted the following report, which was read by Judge Thurman, of the same committee, and was enthusiastically applauded throughout:

TO THE PEOPLE OF OHIO.

In the exercise of the right guaranteed to us by our Federal and State Constitutions, we have this day assembled together, in a peaceable manner, to consult for the common good, and rejecting all mere partisan feeling, to give that utterance to our earnest and sincere convictions, that the state of the country seems to us to demand.

The history of the Democracy of Ohio is a record of unceasing and unvaried devotion to the Union of the States, ever fulfilling the injunctions of the Father of our country; to "cherish a cordial, habitual, and immovable attachment to it; accustoming themselves to think and speak of it as the palladium of their political safety and prosperity, watching for its preservation with jealous anxiety; discountenancing whatever might suggest even a suspicion that it could, in any event, be abandoned; and indignantly frowning upon the first dawning of every attempt to alienate any portion of our country from the rest, or to enfeeble the sacred ties which link together the various parts."

Incited solely by this love for the Union, and for the country it so signally blessed, and believing with Andrew Jackson, that "the foundations of the Union must be laid in the affections of the people"—"in the security it gives to life, liberty, character and property in every quarter of the country, and in the fraternal attachments which the citizens of the several States bear to one another as members of one political family, mutually contributing to promote the happiness of each other," the Democracy of Ohio have never adopted a sectional platform nor ever cast a sectional vote.

Actuated by this enlarged and elevated spirit of patriotism, and esteeming it no dishonor to perpetuate by compromise and concession a Union that was formed and had hitherto been preserved by those means, and trusting that the power of patriotism might overcome the madness of party, the Democracy of Ohio, in conjunction with the other conservative men of the country, most earnestly sought to avert our present calamities, and preserve the Union by peaceable means.

But when the fell spirit of Abolitionism at the North and Secessionism at the South, disregarding the wishes of the majority of the people of both sections, rendered all efforts for a peaceful adjustment ineffectual; when the integrity of the Union was assailed by force and the country plunged into civil war; when the President declared his intention to maintain the supremacy of the Constitution by arms and to employ them for that purpose alone; the Democracy of Ohio, Union men in war as well as in peace, rallied en masse to the support of the Government. From that day to this they have given to every constitutional measure for the suppression of the rebellion an effective support. In the field they have constituted and yet constitute, a moiety, if not more, of the military quota of the State; and there is scarcely a battle ground that does not bear witness to their heroic devotion to the Union. In the National and State councils, they have granted without hesitation all the men and money demanded by the Government; while as private citizens and voters at the ballot box they have given to it a moral support more powerful by far than was ever before given by a party to an administration elevated to power by political opponents. And now in this sore hour of our country's trial, its motto is, as it ever has been, "To maintain the Constitution and preserve the Union." A party whose whole history is thus signally illustrative of patriotism, a party that has thus sacrificed all mere partisan prejudice and feeling, for the sake of the Republic, needs no defense at our hands against the malignant assaults of its enemies, and is entitled to be heard with thoughtful attention when it proclaims its sentiments,

And the time has come when in our judgment, that proclamation should be respectfully but distinctly and earnestly made.

A little less than a year ago, Congress with an almost entire unanimity, solemnly declared that "Congress, banishing all feeling of mere passion and resentment, will recollect only its duty to the whole country; that this war is not waged on their part in any spirit of oppression, or for any purpose of conquest or subjugation, or purpose of overthrowing or interfering with the rights or established institutions of those States, but to defend and maintain the supremacy of the Constitution, and to preserve the Union with all the dignity, equality and rights of the several States unimpaired; and that as soon as these objects are accomplished the war ought to cease."

We need not remind you with what satisfaction this declaration was hailed in the loyal States; how it served to fill the ranks of the army, to strengthen the hands of the Government, and to infuse spirit and fortitude into the breasts of the loyal men of the South who yet clung to the hope of seeing the Union restored in all its pristine vigor and supremacy. And had there been no departure from the spirit of this declaration; had no doctrines been advanced in high or influential places subversive of the most cherished liberties guaranteed by the Constitution to the people; had there been no corruption so monstrous as to appal the nation by its magnitude, and were there no danger to our institutions to be apprehended in the future and to be carefully guarded against, it would not be necessary for us now to address you.

But the powerful and persistent efforts that have been and are yet being made to convert the war into a mere crusade against slavery; the fearful strides taken by Congress at its present session in that direction, and the yet more alarming measures proposed and warmly advocated; the audacious attempts to overawe the President whenever he hesitated to yield to the demand of the radicals; the unmeasured abuse that has been heaped on almost every General in the field, however meritorious, who has declined to become an emissary of abolitionism; the daily promulgation of doctrines utterly destructive of the Constitution and of civil liberty, and the incessant denunciation of every conservative man however loyal, who does not subscribe to them; all give a warning that ought not to pass unheeded by the people, and require of all who desire to see the Constitution maintained and the Union perpetuated, an expression of their sentiments.

We, therefore, the representatives of nearly or quite 200,000 voters of the State of Ohio, who have as deep a stake in the welfare of the country and in the preservation of the Union, as any other equal number of men, in the exercise of our duty and constitutional rights, and with the desire of upholding instead of weakening the just powers of our Government, and anxious to unite all men, without regard to their former party associations, who agree with us in opinion, and to treat all loyal men who honestly differ from us with becoming respect, do hereby declare our own opinions and those of our constituents, as follows:

1. *Resolved*, That we are, as we ever have been, the devoted friends of the Constitution and the Union, and we have no sympathy with the enemies of either.

2. That every dictate of patriotism requires that, in the terrible struggle in which we are engaged for the preservation of the Government, the loyal people of the Union should present an unbroken front; and therefore all efforts to obtain, or perpetuate party ascendency by forcing party issues upon them that necessarily tend to divide and distract them, as the Abolitionists are constantly doing, are hostile to the best intererts of the country.

3. That the Abolition party, by their denunciation of the President whenever he has manifested a conservative spirit, by their atrocious defamation of our Generals who were exposing their lives for their country, and who needed and merited its hearty support, by their acts and declarations tending to promote insubordination in our armies, and a want of confidence in their commanders, and by their persistent representations of all conservative men in the loyal States, as sympathisers with the rebels, have given immense aid and comfort to the rebel cause, and encouraged them to hope for ultimate success.

4. That we have seen with indignation the intimation of the Governor of Massachusetts, that that State will be slow in furnishing her quota of troops, unless the war be carried on for purposes of emancipation. When the nation is straining every nerve, and pouring out its blood and treasure like water, to preserve its existence, it is monstrous that a conditional Unionism that places Abolitionism above the Constitution and the success of a party above the integrity of the Republic, should thus rear its head in high places and seek to dictate the conduct of the war.

5. That while we would mete out merited and legal punishment to the plotters of, and leaders in, the rebellion, we are opposed to the contemplated sweeping and indiscriminate acts of confiscation and emancipation, by Congressional legislation or Executive proclamation, because:

1st. We do not believe such acts would be constitutional.

2d. We believe that by driving the rebels to desperation, and converting Union men at the South into rebels, would have the effect to indefinitely prolong the war, afford a pretext for foreign intervention and render the restoration of the Union next to or quite impossible.

3d. Because, if practicable and carried out they would engender a feeling of bitterness between the different sections of the Union that would not be allayed for generations to come, and that would be an ever-present cause of danger and disturbance to the public peace, a source of perpetual weakness in the Government, and an ever-present incentive to foreign powers to interfere in our domestic concerns, and to promote a disruption and overthrow of the Republic.

4th. Because they would destroy, in a great degree, if not entirely, for many years to come, the industrial interests of a large section of the country, and most injuriously effect the interests of the whole people.

5th. Because the immediate and indiscriminate emancipation of the slaves would be an act of inhumanity to them.

6th. Because such an emancipation would throw upon the border free States and especially upon Ohio, an immense number of negroes to compete with, and underwork, the white laborers of the State, and to constitute, in various ways, an almost, or quite, unbearable nuisance, if suffered to remain among us. And we would deem it most unjust to our gallant soldiers to see them compelled to free the negroes of the South and thereby fill Ohio with a degraded population to compete with these same soldiers upon their return to the peaceable avocations of life.

6th. That entertaining these views, we cannot too strongly condemn the refusal of our General Assembly to prohibit by law, the immigration of negroes into this State.

7th. That we are opposed to being taxed to purchase the freedom of negro slaves. With all due respect to the opinions ot others, we think that such a measure would be unconstitutional, impolitic and unjust.

8th. That the unparalleled frauds and peculations upon the government, revealed by the investigating committees, and otherwise, demand the sternest condemnation of every honest man and friend of the country, and call for the severest punishment prescribed by the laws.

9th. That the patriotism, courage and skill manifested by our armies has never been exceeded in the history of the world, and deserves and receives our highest admiration and gratitude.

10th. That the refusal of the General Assembly to permit our gallant soldiers in the field the right to vote, was a great and unjustifiable wrong to them, that ought not to have been committed.

11th. That while we will, as heretofore, discourage all mere factious opposition to the Administration, and will continue to give our earnest support, to all proper measures to put down the rebellion, and will make all the allowances that the necessities of the case require of good citizens, we protest against all violations of the Constitution.

12th. That we hold sacred, as we do all other parts of that instrument, the following provisions of the Constitution ot the United States:

"The trial of all crimes, except in cases of impeachment, shall be by jury, and such trial shall be held in the State where the said crimes shall have been committed.

"Congress shall make no law respecting an establishment of religion, or prohibiting the free exercise thereof; or abridging the freedom of speech, or of the press; or the right of the people peaceably to assemble, and to petition the government for a redress of grievances.

"The powers not delegated to the United States by the Constitution, nor prohibited by it to the States, are reserved to the States respectively, or to the people.

"The right oi the people to be secure in their persons, houses, papers and effects against unreasonable searches and seizures, shall not be violated, and no warrant shall issue but upon probable cause, supported by oath or affirmation, and particularly describing the place to be searched and the persons and things to be seized.

"No person shall be held to answer for a capital or otherwise infamous crime, unless on a presentment or indictment of a grand jury, except in cases arising in the land and naval forces, or in the militia, when in actual service, in time of war and public danger; nor to be deprived of life, liberty, or property, without due process of law; nor shall private property be taken for public use without just compensation.

"In all criminal prosecutions the accused shall enjoy the right to a speedy and public trial by an impartial jury of the State and District wherein the crime shall have been committed, which District shall have been previously ascertained by law; and to be informed of the nature and cause of the accusation; to be confronted with the witnesses against him; to have compulsory process for obtaining witnesses in his favor, and to have the assistance of counsel for his defense."

And we utterly condemn and denounce the repeated and gross violation by the Executive of the United States, of the said rights thus secured by the Constitution; and we also utterly repudiate and condemn the monstrous dogma that in time of war the Constitution is suspended, or its powers in any respect enlarged beyond the letter and true meaning of that instrument.

13th. That we view with indignation and alarm the illegal and unconstitutional seizure and imprisonment, for alleged political offenses, of our citizens without judicial process in States where such process is unobstructed, but by Executive order, by telegraph or otherwise, and call upon all who uphold the Union, the Constitution and the laws, to unite with us in denouncing and repelling such flagrant violation of the State and Federal Constitutions and tyrannical infraction of the rights and liberties of American citizens; and that the people of this State cannot safely and will not submit to have the freedom of speech and freedom of the press, the two great and essential bulwarks of civil liberty, put down by unwarranted and despotic exertion of power.

After the thanks of the Convention were voted the Committee on Resolutions, for the able and satisfactory manner in which they had discharged the duty that had been assigned to them, loud and continuous calls were made for Mr. VALLANDIGHAM; and when he ascended the platform he was greeted with rapturous cheers. He spoke as follows:

Mr. President, and fellow Democrats of the State of Ohio: I am obliged again to regret that the lateness of the hour precludes me from addressing you, either in the manner or upon the particular subjects which otherwise I should prefer. This is my misfortune again to-day as last night: but speaking thus without premeditation, and upon such matters chiefly as may occur to me at the moment, if I should happen to get fairly under headway, it may turn out to be your misfortune. [Laughter.]

I congratulate the Democracy of Ohio, that in the midst of great public trial and calamity, of persecution for devotion to the doctrines of the fathers who laid deep and strong the foundations of the Constitution and the Union under which this country has grown great and been prosperous—the fathers, by whose principles one and all, the party to which we are proud to belong has always been guided—today we have assembled in numbers greater than at any former convention in Ohio. I congratulate you that despite the threats which have been uttered and the denunciations which have been poured out upon that time-honored and most patriotic organization, peaceably and in quiet, with enthusiasm and earnestness of purpose, we are here met; and in harmony, which is the secret of strength and the harbinger of success, have discharged the duties for which we were called together. There was a time when it was questionable if in free America—in the United States—boasting of their liberties for more than eighty years—a party to which this country is indebted for all that is great and good and grand and glorious—would have been permitted peaceably to assemble to exercise its political rights and perform its appropriate functions. Threats have even been made in times more recent, that this most essential of all political rights, secured to us by the precious blood of our fathers in a seven years' revolutionary war, should no longer be enjoyed. The Democrats of our noble sister State of Indiana, second born daughter of the Northwest, have been menaced within the last ten days, with a military organization and the bayonet, to put down their party. I hold in my hand a telegraphic dispatch from the capital of that State, boasting of this infamous purpose. I will read it, gentlemen; because I know that the same dastardly menaces have been proclaimed against the Democrats of Ohio, and because I am here to day to rebuke them as becomes a free-born man who is resolved to perish—[Great applause, in the midst of which the rest of the sentence was lost.]

Some months ago a Democratic State Convention was held in Indiana. It was a Convention of the party founded by Thomas Jefferson, built up by a Madison and a Monroe, and consolidated by an Andrew Jackson [applause]—a party under whose principles and policy from thirteen States, we have grown to thirty-four; for thirty-four there were, true and loyal to this Union before the Presidential election of 1860—a party under whose wise and liberal policy the course of empire westward did take its way, until the symbol of American power—the stars and stripes—waved proudly from the Atlantic to the Pacific, over the breadth of a whole continent—a party which, by peace and compromise, and through harmony, wisdom and sound policy, brought us up from feeble and impoverished colonies, struggling in the midst of defeat and disaster in the war of the Revolution, to a mighty empire, foremost among the powers of the earth, the foundations of whose greatness, were laid, broad and firm, in that noble Constitution and that grand old Union which the Democratic party has ever maintained and defended. The Democratic party, with such principles and such a history and record to point to, held a State Convention in pursuance of its usages for more than thirty years, and under the rights secured by a State and Federal Constitution older still, in the capital of the State of Indiana. And yet, referring to this party and its Convention, the correspondent of a disloyal and pestilent, but influential newspaper in the chief city of Ohio, dared to send over the telegraphic wires, wires wholly under the military control of the administration which permits nothing to be transmitted not acceptable to its censors, a dispatch in these words:

"The fellows are frightened, evidently not without cause."

Well, gentlemen, I know not how far Democrats of Indiana may be frightened—and a nobler and more fearless body of men never lived—but I see thousands of Democrats before me to whom fear and reproach are alike unknown. Frightened at what? Frightened by whom? We are made of sterner stuff.

"The militia of the State," he adds, "will probably be put upon a war footing very shortly."

And who, I pray, are the militia of the State? They are not made up of the leaders of the Republican party in Indiana or Ohio, I know. I never knew that sort of politicians to go into any such organization, in peace or in war. No men have ever been more bitter and unrelenting in their opposition to and ridicule of the militia; and none knows it better than I, as my friend before me by his smile reminds me that one of my own offenses is that I am a militia brigadier in favor of the next foreign war.

But who are the militia? They are the free-born, strong-armed, stout-hearted Democrats of Indiana as they are of Ohio. Let them be put on a war footing. Good! We have hosts of them in the army already, and on a war footing, but who are as sound Democrats and as much devoted to the principles of the party as they were the hour they enlisted. They have been in the South, and I have the authority of hundreds of officers and privates in that gallant army, for saying that not only are the original democrats in it, more devoted to the party to-day than ever before, but that hundreds also who went hence Republicans, have returned or will return, cured of the disease. [Laughter and applause.] Sir, the army is, fortunately, most fortunately for the country, turning out to be a sort of political hospital or sanitary institution, and I only regret that there are not many more Republican patients in it [Laughter.]

Well, put the militia upon a war footing. Put arms in their hands. They never can be made the butchers or jailors of their fellow citizens, but the guardians rather of free speech and a free press, and of the ballot box. Standing armies of mercenaries, not the militia of a country, are the customary instruments of tyranny and usurpation.

But this correspondent proceeds:

"If the sympathizers with treason and traitors—"

We sympathize with treason and traitors! We, who have stood by the Constitution and the Union from the organization of the party, in our fathers' day and in our own day, in every hour of trial, in peace and in war, in victory and in defeat, amid disaster and when prosperity beamed upon us—we to be branded as enemies to our country, by those whose traitor-fathers burned blue lights as signals for a foreign foe, or met in Hartford Convention to plot treason and disunion fifty years ago! We false to the constitution and to our government, the bones of whose fathers lie buried on every battle field of the war of 1812, from the massacre at the River Raisin to the splendid victory at New Orleans: we who bore aloft the proud banner of the Republic and planted it in triumph upon the palace of the Montezumas: We by whose wisdom in council and courage in the field for seventy years, the Constitution and the Union and the country which has grown great under them, have been preserved and defended; we o be denounced as sympathizing with treason and traitors, by the men who for twenty years have labored day and night for the success of hose principles and of that policy and that party which are now destroying the grandest Union, the noblest Constitution and the fairest Country on the globe! Talk to me about sympathizing with disunion, with treason and with traitors! I tell you, Men of Ohio, that n six months, in three months, in six weeks it may be, these very men and their masters in Washington whose bidding they do, will be the advocates of the eternal dissolution of this Union; and denounce all who oppose it as enemies to the peace of the country. Foreign intervention and the repeated and most serious disasters which have lately bafallen our arms, will speedily force the issue of separation and southern independence—*disunion*—or of Union by negotiation and compromise. Between these two I am—and I here publicly proclaim it—for the Union, the whole Union and nothing less, if by any possibility I can save it; if not, then for so much of it as can yet be rescued and preserved; and in any event and under all circumstances, for the Union which God ordained, of the Mississippi Valley and all which may cling to it, under the old name, the old Constitution and the old flag, with all their precious memories, with the battle fields of the past and the songs and the proud history of the past—with the birth place and the burial place of Washington the founder and Jackson the preserver of the Constitution as it is and of the Union as it was. [Great applause.]

But this correspondent again proceeds:

"If the sympathizers with treason and traitors intend to carry out their plans in this quarter—"

What plans? Just such as to-day have been the business of this Convention; the plans of that old Union party, laying down a platform and nominating Democrats to fill the offices and control the policy of the government, to the end that the Constitution may be again maintained, the Union restored, and peace, prosperity and happiness once more drop healing from their wings.

"Plans," the fellow proceeds, "in this quarter, they will doubtless find the work quite as hot as they bargained for."

And I tell the cowardly miscreant who telegraphed the threat that he and those behind him, will find the work fifty fold hotter when they begin it, than they had reckoned on, both here and in Indiana.

"Ten thousand stand of arms," he adds, "have been ordered for the State troops."

For what? To put down the Democratic party. Sir, that is a work which cannot be done by ten, or twenty or fifty thousand stand of arms in the hands of any such dastards, in office or out of it. If so full of valor and so thirsty for blood, let them enlist under the call just issued for troops in Ohio and Indiana. Let them go down and fight the armies of the "rebels" in the South, and let Democrats fight the unarmed but more insidious and dangerous Abolition rebels of the North and West, through the ballot box.

Forty thousand additional troops, I estimate it, are called for in the proclamation of yesterday, from the State of Ohio. Where are the forty thousand Wide Awakes of 1860, armed with their portable lamp posts,and drilled to the music of the Chicago platform? Sir, I propose that thirty-five thousand of them be conscripted forthwith. They will never enlist; they never do. They are "Home Guards." They "don't go," but stay vigorously at home to slander and abuse and threaten Democrats whose fathers or brothers or sons are in the Union armies or have fallen in battle. I speak generally—certainly there are exceptions. But I will engage that if the records of the old Wide Awake clubs in the several cities and towns of Ohio shall be produced and the Republicans will detail or draft thirty-five thousand from the lists, I will find five thousand strong-armed, stout-hearted, brave and loyal Democrats to go down and see that they don't run away at the first fire. [Great laughter.]

Sympathizers with treason and traitors! Secessionists! Sir, it is about time that we had heard the last of this. The Democracy of Ohio and of the United States, are resolved that an end shall be put to this sort of slander and abuse. But I do not propose to discuss this particular subject further now. [Go on, go on.]

Well, then, from that which concerns the Democratic party, to a word, a single word, about what relates to myself; and I beg pardon for the digression. I am rejoiced that it has been permitted to me to be here present to-day in person before you. Had you believed the reports of the Republican press, you would no doubt have expected to see probably the most extraordinary compound of leprous and unsightly flesh and blood ever exhibited. [Laughter] Well, my friends, you see that I am not quite "monstrous" at least, and bear no especial resemblance to the beast of the Apocalypse, either in heads or horns; but am a man of like fashion with yourselves. To the Republican party alone, and its press and its orators, I am indebted, no doubt, for a large part of the "curiosity" which I am sorry to say, I seem to have excited; and which has brought out even some of them as if to "see the elephant." They have never meant to be friendly towards me, I know; but as I see some of them now within my vision, let me whisper in their ears, that I never had better friends, and no man ever had since the world began. They have advertised me free of cost, absolutely free of cost, for the last fifteen months; yes, I may say for some five years past, all over the United States. Why sir, a Republican editor without "the undersigned" for a text, would be the most unhappy mortal in the world. Every little "printer's devil" in the office would be hollowing for copy, and no copy to be had. I know that they are friends, by the usual sign, "the remarks they make." Gentlemen I have had my share of what Jefferson called the unction, the holy oil with which the Democratic priesthood has always been annointed—slander, detraction and calumny without stint. Really I am not sure that with me it has not reached "extreme unction," though I am by no means ready and do not mean to depart yet. Well, I will not complain. It has cost me not a single night's loss of sleep from the beginning. My appetite, if you will pardon the reference—if you will allow me, as Lincoln would say, to "blab" upon so delicate a subject—has been in no degree impaired by it. Others before me and with me, have endured the same. Here is my excellent friend near me, [Mr. Medary.] Oh blessed Martyr! [Great laughter and applause.] For one and sixty years, the storms of partisan persecution and malignity in every form, have beaten upon his head; but though time and toil have made it gray, the heart beneath beats still to-day, as sound and true to its instincts of Democracy and patriotism, and of humanity too, as when he laid his first offerings upon the altar of his country just forty years ago. What others have heroically suffered in ages past, we, too, can endure.

We are all, indeed, still in the midst of trials. Here before me, is the gentleman of whom I have just spoken, whom you have honored with the Presidency of this noble Convention, for forty years a Democratic editor—for forty years devoted to the Constitution and the Union of these States—a man who, through evil and through good report, has adhered with the faith of a devotee and the firmness of a martyr, to the principles and policy of that grand old party of the Union; and now that the frosts of three score years have descended and whitened his head—he, I say, has lived to see the paper to which he gives the labor and the wisdom of his declining years, prohibited from circulation through a part of the mails, as "disloyal" to the Government! (Cries of no, no, shame.) Samuel Medary disloyal! and Wendell Phillips a patriot! Sir, it is not many months since, that in the city of Washington, in that magnificent building erected by the charity of an Englishman who loved America—I would there were more like him—that art and science might the more widely flourish in this country—the Smithsonian Institute—Wendell Phillips addressed an assemblage of men as false to the Union and the Constitution as himself. Upon the platform was the Speaker of the House of Representatives, the third officer in the Government; by his side the Vice President of the United States, and between these two, in proportions long drawn out, the form of "Honest Old Abraham Lincoln." Am I mistaken, and was it at another and earlier abolition lecture by that other disunionist, Horace Greeley, in the same place—there have been many of them—that Lincoln attended? The Speaker and the Vice President I know were there; and with these two or three witnesses before him, and in presence of the priesthood of Abolitionism, the Sumners and Wilsons, the Lovejoys and the Wades of the House and Senate, (great laughter and cheers,) surrounded by these, the very architects of disunion, he proclaimed that "for nineteen years he had labored to take nineteen States out of the Union" And yet this most spotted traitor was pleading for disunion in the City of Washington, where women are arrested for the wearing of red, white and red upon their bonnets, and babes of eighteen months are dragged from the little willow wagons drawn by their nurses, because certain colors called seditious are found upon their swaddling clothes! The next day, or soon after, this same Wendell Phillips did dine with or was otherwise entertained by his Excellency the President of the United States, who related to him one of his choicest anecdotes. Yet Democratic editors, Democratic Senators and

Representatives, and those holding other official positions by the grace of the States or of the people, are "traitors" forsooth, because they would adhere to the principles and organization of their noble and patriotic old party! Such are some of the exhibitions which Washington has witnessed during the past winter.

Congress, too, has been in session. Sir, I saw it announced in one of the disloyal papers of this city yesterday that Jeff. Davis, and Toombs, and Yancey, and Rhett, and other secessionists of the South, would derive much comfort from this day's meeting. Well, sir, I have just come from a body of men which I would not for a moment pretend to compare for statesmanship, respectability or patriotism, with this Convention. That body has devoted its time and attention to doing more in six months, for the cause of secessionism, than Beauregard, and Lee, and Johnston, and all the Southern Generals combined, have been able to accomplish in one year. Said a Senator from the South, the other day, a Union man: "Jeff. Davis is running two Congresses now, and is making a d—d sight more out of the Washington Congress than the one at Richmond." [Laughter, and many remarks of approval.]

Sir, the legislation of that body has been almost wholly for the "almighty African." From the prayer in the morning—for, gentlemen, we are a pious body, we are—making long faces, and sometimes wry faces, too, (laughter,)—we open with prayer but there is not much of the Almighty Maker of heaven and earth in it—from the prayer, to the motion to adjourn, it is negro in every shape and form in which he can by any possibility be served up. But it is not only the negro inside of the House and Senate, but outside also. The city of Washington has, within the past three weeks, been converted into one universal hospital; every church, except one for each denomination, has been seized for hospital purposes; but while the sanctuaries of the ever living God—the God of Abraham, Isaac and Jacob—not the new God of the Burlingames and Sumners and other Abolitionists, not that God whose gospel is written in the new Bible of Abolition—but the Ever-living Jehovah God, have been confiscated for hospitals, every theatre, every concert saloon, every other places of amusement, from the highest to the lowest—from the spacious theatre in which a Forest exhibits to an enraptured audience his graphic renderings of the immortal creations of Shakespeare, down to the basest den of revelry and drunkenness, is open still; as in the Inferno of the great Italian poet—

"The gates of hell stand open night and day."

Sir, if these places of amusement—innocent some of them, but not holy, certainly—had first been seized as hospitals, for the comfort and cure of the thousands of brave and honest men, who went forth believing in their hearts that they were to battle for the Constitution and the Union, but who now lie wasting away upon their lonely pallets, with no wife, or sister, or mother there to soothe, groaning in agony with every description of wound which the devilish ingenuity of man can inflict by weapons whose invention would seem to have been inspired by the very spirit of the author of all human woe and suffering—wounds, too, rankling and festering for the want of surgical aid—if those places, I say, had first been seized, and then it had become necessary for the comfort or life of the thousands of other sick and wounded who are borne into the city every day, to occupy the churches of Washington, I know of no better or holier purpose to which they could have been devoted. And now, sir, not far from that stately capitol, within whose marble walls abolition treason now runs riot, is a building, "Green's Row" by name, *rented by the Government*, in which one thousand one hundred fugitive slaves—"contrabands" in the precious slang of the infamous Butler—daily receive the rations of the soldier, which are paid for out of the taxes levied upon the people. One hundred thousand dollars a day are taken from the public treasury for the support of fugitive slaves there and elsewhere; while the army of Shields, and other Union armies in the field, even so late as six weeks ago, marched barefooted, bare-headed, and in their drawers, for many weary miles without so much as a cracker or a crust of bread with which to allay their hunger. Aye, sir, while many a gallant young soldier of Ohio, just blooming into manhood, who heard the cry that went up fifteen months ago, "rally to defend the flag and for the rescue of the capital," and went forth to battle, with honesty in his heart, his life in his hand, with courage in every fiber, and patriotism in every vein, lies wan and sad on his pallet in the hospital, your surgeons are forced to divide their time and care between the wounded soldiers and these vagabond fugitive slaves, who have been seduced or forced from the service of their masters. These things and much more—I have told you not a tithe of all—are done in Washington. We know it there, though it is withheld from the people; and while every falsehood that the ingenuity of man can invent to delude and deceive, is transmitted or allowed by the telegraphic censors of the Administration—themselves usurpers unknown to the Constitution and laws—these facts are not permitted to reach the people of the United States. Your newspapers, the natural watch dogs of liberty, are threatened with suppression if but the half or the hundredth part of the truth be told. And now, too, when but one other means remains for the redress of this and the hundred other political grievances, under which the land groans—party organization and public assemblages of the people—even these, too, are threatened with suppression by armed force. Aye, sir, that very party, which not many years ago, bore upon every banner, the motto, "Free Speech and a Free Press," now day by day forbids the transmission through your mails of the papers from which you derive your knowledge of public events, and which advocate the principles you cherish. And Democratic editors, too, are seized, "kidnapped" in the midnight hour—torn from their families—gagged—their wives with officers over them menacing violence if they but ask one farewell grasp of the hand, one parting kiss—thrust into a close carriage in the felon hour of midnight, and with violence dragged to this Capitol and here forced upon an express train and hurried off to a military fortress of the United States. Yes, Men of Ohio, to a fortress that bears the honored name of that first martyr to American liberty—the Warren of Bunker Hill; or it may be to that other bastile desecrating that other name sacred in American history, and honored throughout the earth—the name of that man who forsook home and gave up rank and title, and in the first flush of youth and manhood came to our shores and linked his fortunes with the American cause—the prisoner of Olmutz, the brave and gallant Lafayette. Aye, freemen of the West, fortresses, bearing these honored names, and meant for the defense of the country against foreign foes, and out of whose casemates bristle cannon planted to hurl death and destruction at armed invaders, echo now with the groans and are watered by the tears—not of men only from States seceded and in rebellion, or captured in war, but from the loyal States of the North and the West and from that party which has contributed nearly three fourths of the soldiers in the field to-day. Are these things to be borne? (Never; no, never.) If you have the spirit of freemen in you, bear them not! (Great applause, and cries of that's it, that's the talk.) What is life worth? What are property and personal liberty and political liberty worth; of what value are all these things, if we, born of an ancestry of freemen, boasting, in the very first hours of our boyhood, of a more extended liberty than was ever vouchsafed to any other people, are to fail now in this the hour of sore trial, to demand and to defend them at every hazard? Freedom of the Press! Is the man who sits in the White House at Washington, and who owes all his power to the press and the ballot, is he now to play the tyrant over us? (No! never, never.) Shall the man who sits at one end of a telegraphic wire in the War Department or the Department of State, a mere clerk it may be, a servant of servants, sit down and by one single click of the instrument, order some minion of his a thousand miles off, to arrest Samuel Medary, or Judge Ranney, or Judge Thurman and hurry them to a bastile? [No; it can't be done; we will never allow it] The Constitution says "no man shall be held to answer for crime except on due process of law." Our fathers, six hundred years ago, assembled upon the plains of Runney Mede in old England, and rescued from tyrant hands, not by arms but by firm resolve, the God-given right to be free. Our fathers, in the time of James I, and of Charles I, endured trial and persecution and loss of life and of liberty, rather than submit to oppression and wrong. John Hampden, glorious John Hampden, the first gentleman of England, arrested upon an illegal executive warrant, went calmly and heroically to the cells of a prison rather than pay twenty shillings of an illegally assessed tax, laid in defiance of the constitution and laws of England, and of the rights and privileges of Englishmen. And all history is full of like examples. William Tell brooked the tyrant's frown in his day and generation, in defence of these same rights, in the noble republic of the Swiss; and that gallant little people, hemmed in among the Alps, though surrounded on every side by despots whose legions numbered more than the whole population of Switzerland, have by that same indomitable spirit of freedom, maintained their rights, their liberties and their independence to this hour. And are Americans now to offer themselves up a servile sacrifice upon the altar of arbitrary power? Sir, I have misread the signs of the times and the temper of the people, if there is not already a spirit in the land which is about to speak in thunder tones to those who stretch forth still the strong arm of despotic power, "Thus far shalt thou come, and no farther. We made you: you are our servants." That, sir, was the language which I was taught to apply to men in office, when I was a youth, or in first manhood and a private citizen, and afterwards when holding office as the gift of the people, to hear applied to me; and I bore the title proudly. And I asked then, as I ask now, no other or better reward than, "Well done, good and faithful servant." [Cries of, "You shall have it; you deserve it."] But to-day, they who are our servants, creatures made out of nothing by the power of the people, whose little brief authority was breathed into their nostrils by the people, would now, forsooth, become the masters of the people; while the organs and instruments of the people—the press and public assemblages—are to to be suppressed; and the Constitution, with its right of petition, and of due process of law and trial by jury, and the laws and all else which makes life worth possessing—are to be sacrificed now upon the tyrant's plea that it is necessary to save the Government, the Union. Sir, we did save theUnion for years—yes, we did. We were the "Union savers," not eighteen months ago. Then there was not an epithet in the whole vocabulary of political billingsgate so opprobrious in the eyes of a Republican when applied to the Democratic party as "Union-shriekers," or "Union Savers." I remember in my own city, on the day of the Presidential election, in 1860—I remember it well, for I had that day traveled several hundred miles to vote for Stephen A. Douglas for the Presidency—that in a ward where the judges of election were all democrats, your patriotic Wide-Awakes, strutting in unctious uniform, came up hour after hour thrusting their Lincoln tickets twixt thumb and finger at the judges, with the taunt and sneer, "*Save the Union; save the Union!*" And yet now forsooth, we are "traitors" and "secessionists!" And old grey bearded and grey headed men who lived and voted in the times of Jefferson and Madison, and Monroe, and Jackson—men who have fought and bled upon the battle field, and who fondly indulged the delusion for forty years that they were patriots, wake up suddenly to-day to find themselves "traitors!"—sneered at, reviled and insulted by stripplings "whose fathers they would have disdained to have set with the dogs of their flocks." Of all these things an inquisition searching and terrible, will yet be made, as sure and as sudden, too, it may be, as the day of judgment. We of the loyal states—we of the loyal party of the country, the Democratic party—we the loyal citizens of the United States, the editors of loyal newspapers—we who gather together in loyal assemblages, like this, and are addressed by truly loyal and Union men as I know you are to-day and at this moment (that's so; that's the truth) we, forsooth, are to be now denied our privileges and our rights as Americans and as freemen; we are to be threatened with bayonets at the ballot-box, and bayonets to disperse Democratic meetings! Again I ask, why do they not take up their muskets and march to the South, and like brave men, meet the embattled hosts of the Confederates in open arms, instead of threatening, craven like, to fight unarmed democrats at home—possibly unarmed, and possibly not. [Laughter and applause, and a remark—"That was well put in."] If so belligerent, so eager to shed that last drop of blood, let them volunteer to reinforce the broken and shattered columns of McClellan in front of Richmond, sacrificed as he has been by the devilish machinations of Abolitionism, and there mingle their blood with the blood of the thousands who have already perished on those fatal battle fields. But no; the whistle of the bullet and the song of the shell are not the sort of music to fall pleasantly upon the ears of this Home Guard Republican soldiery.

With reason, therefore, fellow citizens, I congratulate you to-day upon the victory which you have achieved. A great poet has said,

"Peace hath her victories as well as War."

To-day the cause of free government has triumphed. A victory of the Constitution, a victory of the Union, has been won, but is yet to be made complete by the men who go forth from this the first political battle-field of the campaign, bearing upon their banners that noble legend, that grand inscription—THE CONSTITUTION AS IT IS, AND THE UNION AS IT WAS. [Great cheering.] In that sign shall you conquer. Let it be inscribed upon every ballot, emblazoned upon every banner, flung abroad to every breeze, whispered in the zephyr, and thundered in the tempest, till its echoes shall rouse the fainting spirit of every patriot and freemen in the land. It is the creed of the truly loyal Democracy of the United States. In behalf of this great cause it is that we are now, if need be, to do and to suffer in political warfare, whatever may be demanded of freemen who know their rights, and knowing, dare maintain them.—Is there any one man in all this vast assemblage, afraid to meet all the responsibilities which an earnest and inexorable discharge of duty may require at his hands in the canvass before us? (No, no, not one.) If but one, let him go home and hide his head for very shame.

"Who would be a traitor knave,
Who could fill a coward's grave,
Who so base as be a slave,
Let him turn and flee."

It is no contest of arms to which you are invited. Your fathers, your brothers, your sons are already by thousands and hundreds of thousands, on the battle field. To-day their bones lie bleaching upon the soil of every Southern State from South Carolina to Missouri. It is to another conflict, Men of Ohio, that you are summoned, but a conflict, nevertheless, which will demand of you some portion at least, of that same determined courage, that same unconquerable will, that same inexorable spirit of endurance, which make the hero upon the military battlefield. I have mistaken the temper of the men who are here to-day, I have misread the firm purpose that speaks in every eye and beams from every countenance, which stiffens every sinew and throbs in every breast; I have misread it all, if you are not resolved to go home and there maintain at all hazards and by every sacrifice, the principles, the policy and the organization of that party to which again and yet again I declare unto you, this Government and country are indebted for all that have made them grand, glorious and great. [Cheers and great applause.]

Upon the conclusion of Mr. VALLANDIGHAM's speech, loud calls were made for Judge RANNEY, whose appearance on the stand was greeted with applause. He spoke as follows:

Gentlemen—It has just occurred to me that when I appeared here a little while ago to ask a favour of you, viz: to take my name from the list of your nominees, I was uncivil in not thanking you for the partiality you manifested in giving me the nomination unasked for. While, my friends, I do not want your office, I still esteem the favor. I cast my lot with the democratic party of this State before I was a voter, in the good old days of Jackson. I have seen a great deal of the party since that time. It has been kind to me; it has done me a thousand fold more than justice on all occasions, and I beg leave to say that I return you my sincere and unfeigned thanks for this repeated confidence in me. I had hoped, and it is a cause of sincere regret, that it is otherwise, that I could have been left free from any connection with the ticket to be elected this fall. Three years ago you made it my duty, by designating me as your candidate for Governor, to visit many of the counties of the State. I have not seen many of you since; but you will remember that I warned you that fanaticism at both ends of this Union was dragging you on to civil war, bloodshed and destruction. The terrible realization has come upon us; we are in the midst of a horrible war. The startling fact stares us in the face, that hundreds and thousands of our friends on the field of battle—not less than one hundred thousand, have gone to that bourne from whence no traveler returns. One hundred thousand firesides have had the pall of death drawn over them. If we may place confidence in the statement of the Chairman of the Committee of Ways and Means in the House of Representatives, we are in debt already more than one thousand millions of dollars. With the increased debt of Ohio, and our share of the National debt, a mortgage is resting upon the property of the State of not less than one hundred millions of dollars. Is it not time for freemen to ask those in power, Watchman what of the night? Is there treason in that? Let me say to you, my fellow citizens, that great as these sacrifices are, and wonderful as they are, if they are made for the sole purpose of upholding that glorious fabric of government to which Washington put his name, they are not too much. If, on the contrary, this enormous expense is made, and the blood flows, to undermine that glorious old fabric, then every drop of blood that is shed is but infusing poison into the body politic; and every dollar that is contributed goes to forge the chains of yourselves and your children. What then is our plain duty? An Executive is in power that we did not contribute to elect; but he is none the less our Executive; he wields the power of Government, and it is our Government, thank God. We can all prove title to it. If I was to run back my title-deeds, I could go to Bunker Hill and show my ancestors in the first contest for independence. What then have we a right to demand? Plainly and simply that the trumpet now shall give no uncertain sound, and that the Executive shall lift aloft the banner of the Constitution, and go before us, as he was elected to do. Plainly and simply we have right to demand the pillar of cloud by day and of fire by night, that may lead us to the harbor of safety. We have a right to know whether the Government is waging this war to uphold the Constitution and the laws, and to perpetuate the Government our fathers gave us; or, whether it be waged, on the other hand, for the purpose of overturning the institutions of the States, and for the purpose of annulling those guarantees of liberty that our fathers inserted in that instrument.

And now a word as to loyalty. If Abraham Lincoln will just raise aloft the banner of the Constitution, and go before us with it, all that I am and all that is mine, he shall have, if it be the last dollar and drop of blood. But while it is our duty to do this, it is our duty also to tell Mr. Lincoln and that worst Congress that ever assembled, that we fight for the institutions of our fathers—we fight because our laws have been invaded—we fight to put down rebellion, and that laws may have their accustomed sway. We must tell them that we are not fighting for any other thing, or what Congress is looking to. We must tell him that the proud race descended from the freemen of Runny Meade that cleared these forests--that have built up the institutions of the country, the Churches and Schools, that have rolled the tide of population from the Atlantic till it rests on the broad Pacific, let us tell him and them plainly, that that proud race are not prepared to surrender or divide this goodlyland. (Never.) No, we are not prepared to divide this goodly land with the Cannibals that have been imported from the coast of Africa. (Great applause.) It is best to be plain on this subject. I do not care what a man calls himself, I want the substance of things. If there is any man who is willing to stand up for the Constitution, and fight for it, that man is my friend. This country is not going to be divided, my friends. (A voice—The democrats must get into power pretty soon then.) We may in folly and madness continue, God knows how long, to use the bayonet and cut each others throats and oppress ourselves with taxes. I can not tell when this is going to stop. I would as soon bring down the wildest lunatic from the Asylum to tell you, as attempt to tell you myself. But while the waters of the Scioto flow on, and make their way down the currents of the great valleys of the West—rolling until they bury themselves in the blue ocean, throughout all that great extent, the land will be occupied by the same glorious people. To upset or change this order of things—be as foolish as we can, is impossible. God Almighty has bound together this great valley in a way that the folly and madness of man can never disrupt it.

Gentlemen, I am glad I am here—glad I came here—glad to see you all. I am glad, whether weal or of woe may betide us, that this proud meeting of the democracy of this noble State has taken place here to-day.—I believe we came here in the right spirit—forgetting ourselves, and looking only to the bleeding country before us. We come for the purpose of seeing whether those noble old ancestors that three generations ago established their independence, are still remembered, and whether their virtues remain with us. We came here to see whether we could do our mite in giving direction to public affairs, as we their descendants should be able to do—whether we are resolved on maintaining the declaration that these States are and of right ought to be free and independent. And we have discharged our duty well I think.—Mortals are constantly liable to err; and with unintentional errors we know how to get along. I congratulate you, and myself, that in spending this day for our country you have done a deed that, I feel no doubt, when you and I are called to close our mortal career, we can say we look back to with satisfaction; and that our children after us, who are to inhabit this great country, stretching along these mighty rivers, when they read of the history of this day, and read that we took part in it, will rejoice to see that their fathers could stand up in their country's hour of peril, not despairing or giving up for a moment, but rallying to the last for the prosperity and security of their common country.

At the close of Judge Ranney's remarks, Judge Thurman was loudly and continuously called for. At last he reluctantly took the stand and began:

Why, what kind of people are you? [A voice—"white people."] Have you not read in Republican newspapers about Thurman sympathizing with rebels, as well as Vallandigham and Medary, and why do you call on us to speak? [A voice—"We sympathize with you."] Well, I tell you what it is, you had better take care that you are not taken out of your beds and carried off to Fort Warren some of these nights. I would like to make a speech to you, but there is not time now. [Go on; we can stay here all night to hear the truth.] Well, after the two or three regular speeches, you will not want more than a short one from me.

This shall be my text: That never, since God made this world, has any party been so infamously treated as has the Democratic party since this war began. [That's true.] Never, since history began to be written, was there a party that made the same sacrifices of its feelings, prejudices and opinions, and brought its influence to bear so strongly in support of an administration that it didn't elect and elevate to power, as has the Democratic party since the war began. And what has been the return? We had done all we could to avert the war; not one of us had uttered one word in favor of secession; not one of us had ever made an argument in favor of the dissolution of the Union. On the contrary, we had stood for the Union under circumstances that would have almost justified us in cutting loose from all sympathies with the South; they had treated us—the Democratic party in the North—with something less than respect, at the Conventions in Charleston and Baltimore; we had a right to complain of them, but we sacrificed our feelings upon the altar of the country; and remembering our duty to the

Constitution and the Union, we said to those men with whom we had co-operated so long, we will forget our resentments if you will help to save the Union. We remonstrated with the South against secession; we argued with the North against secession; we set our faces against every extreme sentiment or feeling that would lead to alienation. We besought the people to lay aside party feeling and sacrifice everything that stood in the way of the country's welfare, that we might preserve the land from that which we now see has happened to it. That is what we did; and we were treated with scorn and contumely from that time on. Little flippant fellows—not knee high to a duck, as the boys say—would say to old gray haired men, "You don't know anything about this matter; we'll run over the continent in thirty days, and make those fellows skedaddle and behave themselves." There were at the South just as bad a set of men; they were determined to break up the Union; and these two classes played into each other's hands. The Southern party to this disunion platform gave the finishing touch to their work by firing upon Fort Sumter, and then what did the Democratic party do? It gave a support such as no political party ever before gave to an Administration chosen by political opponents. The whole north presented a unanimous front to check the madness of the South. What followed? Why it was not a month before we who had sent our sons and brothers to the field by hundreds of thousands—who were pouring out treasure and blood—were denounced by the Abolitionists as rebel sympathizers, if we would not go the whole abolition figure and make this a war of emancipation. They could not be content with a united North, to restore the Union and maintain the Constitution. That was too Democratic. They were willing to have a united North, but it must be on the Wendell Phillips plan, and every man who would not stand on that platform was a rebel sympathiser. No matter what was his position, if he didn't bow the knee to the black god of Abolition, he was a rebel traitor, or at least a sympathizer with traitors. What General who is a Democrat has not met all kinds of opposition and difficulty? What have they said of McClellan, and what will they say now that misfortune has befallen him? What of Grant, and every other Democratic General you can mention? But if a man will be an abolitionist like Hunter, and put red breeches on niggers, and guns in their hands, and demand the same rights and consideration for them as free white soldiers enjoy—if he be a man like Fremont, that will issue a proclamation that his own commander-in-chief has to revoke, they will applaud and stand by all he does. But if he is a man like Grant, that takes ten thousand rebels at a clip, you are told that he deserves to be hung! Yes, though you give your flesh and blood to put down rebellion, if you do not favor Abolition, you are denounced as a rebel sympathizer.

This injustice has gone on about long enough. [Applause, and cries of "that's so—that's the talk."]

It is time for these denunciations to cease. Abuse of the Northern Democracy and violations of the Constitution, without even the plausible pretext of public necessity, are poor modes of strengthening the arm of the Government. When this great Government, with 700,000 troops at its back, takes a little village editor of Ohio, at midnight, out of his bed, and sends him seven hundred miles away to a political Bastile, for a mere expression of opinion, however erroneous; when this is done without even the semblance of legal process, and in a State where the courts are all open and unobstructed, in a state whose loyalty it is infamous to doubt, and where the man could do no harm to the nation even had he tried; why what have we come to? What a scene is this in one of the mightiest nations on the face of the earth! A poor little country editor, with a neighborhood circulation of a few hundreds for his paper, is arrested and sent to Fort Warren on a pretext of enmity to the Union, and upon a plea of public necessity, while Wendell Phillips, who boasts of his disunionism for nineteen years, and who denounces the war as infamous unless it be carried on for purposes of emancipation, perambulates the country at will, giving utterance to his disloyalty, and is feted and lionized at the National Capitol. You have this day again solemnly declared your intention to support the Government in all proper measures to put down the rebellion; but you protest against violations of the Constitution and infringements of the rights and liberties of the people; and you think, as I think, that it is time that injustice to loyal men should stop. [Applause.]

Upon the conclusion of Judge Thurman's speech, the Convention adjourned, with three cheers for the nominees, three for the Convention, and three for the Union.

THE EVENING OF THE FOURTH.

Soon after dark, a large assemblage of the people from all parts of the State, gathered in the street in front of the Goodale House, and remained until midnight, listening to able and eloquent speeches delivered by Messrs. A. M. Jackson, of Crawford; J. H. Train, of Jefferson; State Senators Kinney, of Ashland, and Finck, of Perry; and Congressmen Vallandigham, of the 3d, and White, of the 6th districts.

All the speeches were good, and several of them were such as are seldom surpassed. The great issues of the hour were discussed n a spirit which showed that the hearts of he speakers were in the words they uttered.

The enthusiasm of the people was unounded, and frequent cheers rent the air, s some sentiment of unfaltering devotion o the Constitution and the Union, or some atriotic appeal to stand by the old Government established and maintained by Vashington, Jefferson and Jackson, burst rom the orators' lips. The tones of the peeches, and the echoing responses of the udience, were an earnest of that Demoratic thunder that will roll through the alleys and over the hills of Ohio next ll, causing Abolition Disunionism to ide its diminished head.

ORGANIZATION OF THE DEMOCRATIC STATE CENTRAL COMMITTEE.

COLUMPUS, JULY 4, 1862.

At a meeting of the State Central Committee held in room No. 18, American Hotel, Columbus, Ohio, July 4th, 1862, a permanent organization was effected by electing James McKinney, Esq., of Steubenville, Chairman, and R. K. Cox, jr., of Cincinnati, Secretary.

On motion it was carried that an Executive Committee of five be appointed to act in conjunction with this Committee.

The following were appointed: Col. Samuel Medary, Amos Layman and Jacob Reinhard, of Columbus; J. F. Bollmeyer, of Dayton, and Arthur Hughes, of Cleveland.

The following resolution was offered by Dr. George Fries and unanimously adopted, to wit:

Resolved, That we respectfully recommend to the Democratic Executive Committee of each and every county in the State to call general county meetings at their earliest convenience, to respond to the action of the State Convention, held this day, and to transact such other business as may be conducive to the best interests of the Democratic party in their respective counties.

On motion, adjourned to meet at the same place on the 21st of August next, at 10 o'clock, A. M.

R. K. Cox, Jr.
Secretary of State Central Committee.

PROCEEDINGS OF THE CONVENTION.

We are prepared to furnish pamphlet copies of the Proceedings of the hio Democratic State Convention at the following rates:

INGLE COPY	$ 10
WELVE COPIES	1.00
IXTY COPIES	3.00
NE HUNDRED COPIES	4.00
IVE HUNDRED COPIES	10.00
NE THOUSAND COPIES	18.00

Address, BOLLMEYER & LOGAN,

Publishers EMPIRE, Dayton.

www.ingramcontent.com/pod-product-compliance
Lightning Source LLC
LaVergne TN
LVHW020634110826
845149LV00004B/1179